THE GATHERING

poems by

Morgan Baylog Finn

Finishing Line Press
Georgetown, Kentucky

THE GATHERING

ACKNOWLEDGMENTS

"Guernica" in *PMS* (*poetrymemoirstory*)
"Downpour, 4:00 A.M." in *Castings*, and on *Art in the Air Poetry Contest* (radio program)
"The Gathering" (as "Insubstantial Women"), and "Last Photograph of Grandmother Maria" in *Embers*
"The Fruit Cellar" as a CPTV video, and in *Thema and Castings*
"The Minister's Wife," "Viewing Sweet Peas and Their Absence Acutely," "On the Way to Pump Iron at Tully's," and "Davida and I Check Out Saks," in *Kalliope*
"Double Breech Birth" in *Giving Birth to Ourselves*
"Applying TV Makeup to a CEO" in *Crab Creek Review*
"Thaw" in *Long River Run* (published by The Connecticut Poetry Society)
"I Drive Through Canaan to Shagroy Market" in *Castings*; WEN first prize winner*
"The Makeover Party" in South Florida Review
"To Mother, Age 76, as She Sky-dives," WEN, 1ST prize winner*
*(Writers-Editors Network International Writing Competition)

Publisher: Leah Huete de Maines
Editor: Christen Kincaid
Cover Art: Mysticsartdesign, Pixabay
Author Photo: Michael Fink
Cover Design: Elizabeth Maines McCleavy

Order online: www.finishinglinepress.com
also available on amazon.com

Author inquiries and mail orders:
Finishing Line Press
PO Box 1626
Georgetown, Kentucky 40324
USA

Contents

Doesn't everything die at last, and too soon?
Tell me, what is it you plan to do
with your one wild and precious life?
—Mary Oliver
"The Summer Day"

GUERNICA

Picasso furiously painted his huge black, white and gray mural in six weeks for the 1937 World's Fair after Hitler's Luftwaffe used the tiny defenseless Basque hamlet as a bombing experiment on a packed market day, killing women, children, the elderly, even animals in the field as they fled.

I. WOMAN WITH THE LANTERN

Never again will I lean from my window
and believe an orderly mind
can hold back sorrow. Instead,
I will live out my days wearing weeds.
Assemblymen who swore beneath our ancient oak tree
to protect us, lay scattered in pieces . . .
clergy blood colors the soil;
Ah, Miguel, our Archangel, avenge us!
Yet if Napoleon, if even the Moors
could not break us, neither will Franco.

What's done is done, *mis caros.*
For now, weep and curse fate.
Then pull the edges together.
To endure, pretend a little, nod vaguely.
If I could, I would gather you to me,
reminding you as my own children
that we must go on. Always there are angels
and other lanterns. Haven't you heard
how, mid-dirge, the *Gernikako Arbola,*
our sacred oak, has not fallen?

II. THE DESPAIRING WOMAN

Has anyone seen my little Cecelia—
her footsteps full of
hesitation—not tripping over rubble,
but grabbing the air as if
she might? Because of her illness,
whose name moves over my tongue like sour milk,
we honored her Saint's Day early.

Even on this street of corpses,
I could spot her pale hands,
tapered as fish at market,
fingers coming to life
as she makes bread,
their clumsiness hidden in dough.
But her short vision makes our courtyard
seem to her more than gray buildings
held together by clotheslines and rumor.
For Cecelia, the giving dough is enough,
and the embrace of clean sheets,
though who knows for certain
what she kneads and gathers in.

Blessed Mother, since her birth
my brow has crinkled from praying
to Santa Lucia, the virgin, to Santa Bernardina.
Please do not let this be their reply: Cecelia
snatched from me, no bread
for our table, laundry fluttering
until morning.

III. THE SPEARED HORSE

My hooves clattered a warning on cobblestones,
but your denial kept blocking it out.
Listen!
Must martyred saints scratch
at your doors? Or do you think
my bowed back can carry you
to safety?

From the stable I felt
death straining and refused
to come out. Beatings from drunk masters
are better than bowels rotting in the arena,
or being herded to market. It is never
prudent to sleep lying down.

The earth waits, the earth wishes
to swallow my cry,
but this is not the first time
I've been brought to my knees,
tongue protesting.

IV. THE VICTIM OF FLAMES

Even now, Mama, you draw
your shawl around many sorrows,
yet turn away from me.
Years I tried to make up for what my presence
does to you, kneeling
for your absolution
before Holy Communion,
but the slash of your mouth only tightened,
causing me to run by your clock after marriage,
my words out of sequence when my husband
tried to unbraid my hair, mine the last lamp
burning in the courtyard hours after
Javier stopped calling me to bed—
so that mornings he wandered outside to test
oak trees for warp as I spewed from the window:
"Can your fine ships keep our skies from exploding?"
as he slumped off to butt planks, and I
kept scrubbing even that high window
nobody can see, while sputtering
to clotheslines and chickens, pausing only to
pay my respects to the dead,
screeching afterward to Javier
about who would be next—until I
finally slept . . . oh, but Mama,
when I glanced away from the clock
I felt your hands striking . . . if only
you had embraced me just once,
I would have burst into five constant stars
of white, pink, blue, green, and yellow,
this wound of a mouth healed.

V. THE DISMEMBERED WARRIOR

Filled with its own thoughts, my head
never belonged to this body—any more
than the moon is part of the Pyrenees.
Head often floating outdoors,
teeth clamped on a cigar,
my face would peer through a window
at my poor Jacinta having one of her fits
as she screamed at me to do this
and do that until wine
made her pass out mid-scream.

Only then could I focus
on matador dreams
of how to stop German bombs.
Long before I raised
the Basque sword against fascists,
perhaps I would have made a good priest
had my first vision of Jacinta
not cut with such a hot edge
through my prayers. Yet even at our wedding,
I saw her petals start falling.

El Toro, with the vigilant eyes—
when my Jacinta beats out her grief
on your vast shoulders, please tell her about
the flower blooming from my broken sword.

VI. THE LAMENTING MOTHER

When my daughter greeted me crying,
I refused food—until my milk ebbed.
Nothing tempted, not even those big purple grapes
I craved while pregnant—back when I still
slept and sang, Manuel's hand on my belly.

Mother of God, what is wrong with me?
None of my sisters swore at their infants
when they whined away nights, but I fermented,
shaking my baby the way a dog shakes rabbits,
spewing taunts like in the gypsy *soledades*:
>   *Your father bounces you on his knee.*
>   *Tell me the last time he held me.*
>   *Hungry again, my bawling daughter?*
>   *Here let my fists feed you,*
>   *let them turn you the purple of grapes.*

When the bells of Santa Maria chimed,
followed by guttural sounds,
I thought anything louder than
what shrieked inside me must be a sign.
Bravo, the pigeons are migrating early! I cried,
praying that our men would return
from the Bilbao front to snare them
with a net. Except rubble and flame rained
on us. Releasing a tiny sigh, my child went limp
as a pigeon at market. I implored El Toro for mercy,
but He turned away from me
as a sky full of roaring falcons swooped
down—until it was all the same to me:
pigeons and falcons, dogs and torn rabbits,
bombers and the sad-eyed Mother of God;
who can escape the net, the net?

VII. THE SURVIVING BULL

Stuff your Oles! and roses,
your pious candles. Look around you,
instead. Basque shrieks have split
the air, leaving behind only corpses, which I
have presented to you as children. Yet
you continue to gawk as if expecting
a curtain to fall, their remains
to jump up for one last curtsy or bow.
Do you imagine I lost sleep
to turn their despair into art
for your entertainment?

Stop smacking your lips
in mock sorrow, secretly glad it's not you.
Shame for slinking around like mongrels,
poking here and there with insatiable fingers,
coaxing my hide to expose old wounds—
any patch of thin skin where the sword
can enter. God knows how long
I have glared across these tablelands,
backed against the Bay of Biscay,
without glancing behind me—except for
an occasional bellow over my shoulder
where some damn fool bird
keeps singing its heart out.

DOWNPOUR, 4 AM

—The earth waits, the earth wishes to swallow my cry . . .
The Speared Horse

When rainfall is this heavy
with no vision between water,
branches reach across back roads
for miles, and green creeps down
curbs as if getting ready
to cross. Once in this gray light,
on the way to bring an attorney
my marriage, from these secretive
woods, a stag vaulted over
blacktop, then vanished into
morning. And, oh, how I ached
to go with him, but even if
there were no appointments
to keep, I was afraid
to follow into that forest
where I'd gone as a child.
Grateful that he'd flung himself
over my day, I forgot
where I was going, what secrets
went with me. By the side of the
road, I held my breath, wishing
for his wary grace—until I bent
my head to the steering wheel
and sobbed for that stag,
I suppose, and whatever else
vaults into morning.

THE GATHERING

—If I could, I would gather you to me . . .
                Woman with the Lantern

They surround the oak sewing machine
Aunt Helen left me, left to her
by my Hungarian grandmother.
Boards missing, the parts came east
blanketed in the trunk of my car,
women's voices wafting in,
wafting out of hot August windows
that whole eternal width of Pennsylvania.
Straining senses, I couldn't gather in
words, but they wept and they shouted,
tears flying across flatlands--
so many birds. The sky darkened.
One of them sang in a grieved coloratura,
notes like snarled thread. By the time
we reached home, they had hurtled
their voices into the trees
and mostly sit staring now
at the black iron treadle,
touching with worked fingers
the gilt Sphinx design--
pressing again and again
their foreheads to the metal.

LAST PHOTOGRAPH OF GRANDMOTHER MARIA

—You draw your shawl around many sorrows.
The Victim of Flames

To which steel mill could you have turned,
holding out despair? Instead,
you took Grandfather's beatings
as if you deserved them, your voice
rising on Sundays only
above the congregation, their eyes
sidelong from gossip. Sepia years
with no heart in them made you lean
too often toward blackberry wine,
little Maria, the bitter. Let me
sit beside you on the porch swing
and unseal your locked hands, Grandmother.
I want to place our secret between them and gaze
beyond the neglected yard, the spindly hollyhocks,
over the steeple of St. Stephan's,
beyond the steel mills that lured
Grandfather out of Budapest,
severing from the concert stage
your coloratura. Help me learn Hungarian,
assertive k-words vaulting fences,
while I touch your face so faded
from the small, dark exclamation
of your wedding portrait.
Buszke sciv (proud heart) *Nagymama!*
Unbow your spine like any hollyhock. Let me overflow
your arms with the bold geraniums you favored,
as we sing along the sidewalks into town,
to face down together the blazing mills,
St. Stephan's curse, our buried secrets.

LEGACY

—My head never belonged to my body . . .
The Dismembered Warrior

Take Grandpa Baylog, for instance:

he kept forever moving
as if the moving were holy,
from decades matching the iron's demands—
its reverberant crimson ragings.
Though his blacksmith muscles only
let him sit down for supper,
when my Hungarian grandfather
ate hot peppers wearing his fedora,
he could rivet my brothers and me to our chairs
with his fierce blackberry eyes,
barbarian tongue staking out silence:
"Hallgass!"
his spectacular mustache dunking
into loud slurps of wine.

He was killed burrowing through
a blizzard with his citizenship papers
two weeks before Christmas,
his wiry body left curbside
to drift over with snow . . .

and I could go on from there.

THE FRUIT CELLAR

—For now, weep and curse fate.
Woman with the Lantern

Bare feet drawn to hard earth
my eyes are new fruit
watching Mother down cellar on Mondays
singsong memos to the washing machine
as it sloshes. Unloading clothes
that smell of harsh soap, she feeds them
piecemeal through the wringer,
squeezing out secrets, dropping everything
lifeless into a tub. Under the dangling bulb
Mother chants, not seeing spider webs
join my shadow elongating itself
toward the fruit cellar door where Grandfather
reached into barrels, choosing apples for me—
the shy child built into his lap.
He pared them with his calm knife,
rosy transparent skins falling
unbroken from his fingers.
Gone! Overnight! Laid out in the parlor,
Grandmother, arthritis knotting her bones,
from her bed sobbing: "Daddy, oh, daddy, why did
you leave me?"—my grandfather's lap
unfolded into the earth. They taught
four-year-old fingers the Twenty-third Psalm,
copied over and over from the big family bible
until I got it right: I shall not want, I will only
creep down splintered steps—
another shadow cast by dim light—
restoring my soul on the perfume of old apples
as my toes dig into dampness.

THE MINISTER'S WIFE

—If only you had embraced me just once . . .
The Victim of Flames

The Four Horsemen are slipping
their boots into stirrups! he stressed.
baptizing my ripe belly right here
under this mural of Jesus ascending—
should Armageddon descend.

Night after night, my husband dissects darkness
behind the heavy oak door of his study,
where he proves that snakes
have laid claim to the soil. Upstairs,
I toss, swatting mosquitoes,
as pig feeder clanks from nearby farms
ride the hours. Pared down to despair,
I've fallen back on devotion:
ever since my husband approached me
in the company of Saint Paul,
I have not cut my hair.

Fascination peeks over my hymnal on Sundays
as he bristles the pulpit, rocks slightly
in his black patent shoes. Pausing long,
pausing often, he sure knows how to give us
a good look at Hell. Migraine or not,
I gulp my prescription,
focusing all the better for it
on those moonstone-blue eyes
that goosebump my spirit as he
convicts us with scripture.

Knuckles white and face florid,
he stares us down slowly,
one at a time: *Do you really believe*
you can whitewash your souls
ONE hour on Sundays? Press your ears
to the earth! Nobody breathes until from troughs,
those relentless hogs reply. The choir
rises fast for the last hymn; they *Hallelujah!*
up the aisle. Lips thinning into a smile,
my flushed reverend strides.

Behind his black swirl of cassock,
my tangle of hair and
blessed body follows.

DOUBLE BREECH BIRTH

For Mary Elisabeth

—Since her birth my brow has crinkled from praying...
The Despairing Woman

You wrenched from my breasts, maroon and screaming,
for staggering months. Brain-damage, they said,
lack of oxygen shattering all dreams
of the dazzling superstar daughter I'd

required. Quite an entrance, screeching like one
who would never fit in—far from my grace,
fallen like a fairy tale frog. Undone,
I nursed migraines with codeine as you raged

seventeen years for my heart, your clumsi-
ness why I tried to makeover the child
who had blundered so awkwardly from me—
until your flaws burrowed into my shame-filled

soul, our mirrored selves binding the lesion.
Little determined gift: my salvation.

VIEWING SWEET PEAS AND THEIR ABSENCE ACUTELY

—What is wrong with me?
        The Lamenting Mother

We used to wade through them,
my skinny kid brothers and I,
past a charred foundation
on the way to our wild apple tree
in the woods, where I vowed they would

fly like Superman, burlap sacks tied
to their bony shoulders, and I got an inkling
of their limits. Our tree is long-gone—
a strip mall rolled over it—gone
the heartwood exposure in its hollow.

And no more pink-white-purple bouquets
for Mother. As if they helped. Nowadays,
her fatigue makes me take long walks
to visit what's left of those woods,
where I wait for its secrets to reach out

and cover me like moss until I learn
how to make her flourish like those pink
and pinker impatiens she plants.
Whatever it takes to release the woman
with sad, penciled brows and vague laughter

from inside her pristine white condo.
Aware that someday she'll be gone—
her phone number assigned to some stranger—
I sell her on each new spit-polished cure
I find, dragging her to this fringe doctor,

and that promise of pep as she murmurs:
"Are you sure *this* will work?"
with such weary suspicion that even if
our apple tree burst through concrete,
and in their fifth decade my brothers

finally flew from it, she would glaze over,
sighing, "What tree?" Mother
and not my mother reminds me
that she avoided those woods;
she knew there'd be snakes.

APPLYING TV MAKEUP TO A CEO

—Thin skin where the sword can enter.
The Surviving Bull

He motions for me to close the door
as I swab astringent that helps seal pores
against hot teleconference lights.
Next, the slathering of foundation
across his beet-red brow—away from
where he's sprayed thinning hair rigid—
to temples where his pulse jars mine,
along cheekbones and bird-nerve lids,
then southward to putty mouth brackets.
He winks at me in the mirror,
thanking god for those on-flight gin and tonics
that jelled his presentation on profit and loss.

I hover above him—
chicken-necked geisha
and broken-nosed godmother—
as if either can handle his wish: no jowls.
When I insist his jawline is fine,
he squints at me like a slow year. I get paid
to listen, to prime a man's face
with hands already leaping to what's
required of them, what just passed
between us, gone. Defining his jaw
with a darker shade, I powder whiskers
that mark implacable time,
numb from touching anybody
this close, this long. I never
read my own babies like this,
their irises and his the same
shattered blue glass.

He sticks out his tongue at the 12-bulb mirror,
you'd almost think he's fine, but for
the boozy smell—cessation of sweat,
our mission. I swab his forehead three times,
shove tissues into damp fists
as he rushes from my appraisal,
his flight reflected in a galley of mirrors . . .

who can endure so much light?

THAW

—Brought to my knees . . .
The Speared Horse

Gray sky, gray fence, gray tree.
Day after day, my communion
of strays take in
        my fatigue at the window,
           the snow-drifted fence,
             a tangle of branches
on my crab-apple tree. My cats
stare unblinking for hours; we'd settle
for the crankiest blue jay back at the feeder.

But this morning I feel the tree's quiet trembling
as it waits. Soon, the irritable snapping of ice
before it releases gray limbs.

By noon, the relentless melting, dripping, plopping
makes us droop like the withered apple
dangling from my grafted tree.

Then as night closes in, I see one cat scale
to the portion of cage rising above
gray fencing where she listens for life
under snow—keeping the watch over
a sliver of pine-green forest—
all greedy gold eyes and ripe senses,
claws stapled to wire.

I CONSIDER WHERE TO BUILD MY CAT CAGE

—Who can escape the net, the net?
The Lamenting Mother

I will begin by caging in the forest,
asking my fence man which wire
outlasts the seasons, allowing branches
their bloom. Cage fairly my portion
of river and sky, I will tell him.
Please gird my cage deep
for when the earth settles.

I will keep paying my fence man
until that cage rises higher
than the tallest pitch pine
topping Bear Mountain,
just barely skimming
the midnight star,
a cage so vast,
my cats won't resent me.
An invisible fortress
where I can leap inside
to follow one cat—
the color of all I've known—
as it bounds across fields
with me following so closely
my neighbors will see

just any old cat and its shadow
stalking the full Harvest Moon.

I DRIVE THROUGH CANAAN TO SHAGROY MARKET

—An occasional bellow . . .
      The Surviving Bull

past cornfields and orchards where rain-boughed trees
touch my car. When I climbed trees and the crazed
wind took me, I felt gloriously free.
Now I brake by penned veal-calves grazing.
If released, where could they go? Just like me
during the decades when I grew dumb-eyed
from devotion to men, from following
numbly—until I forgot how to ride
trees, forgot their salvation, forgot how
storm-winds had taken me in. I yielded
till a girlhood psalm sang me, bawling, toward
light like a calf chuted into a field.

At market let me pass slowly the meats
for wild blackberries, brie, and rye bread.

THE MAKEOVER PARTY

—To endure, pretend a little . . .
Woman with the Lantern

Last Saturday night
at Marty's restored Victorian,
Cassie contoured away excess,
angling in hollows as she hummed to herself.
Swirling again and again her swift powder,
she smiled as she sponged it over,
downsinking our flaws to the ocean floor.
Back and forth we were spun;
had Marty's soprano not grounded us,
we might have—as ancient fish—flown.

But Marty's canvas was stretched
to new limits. Cassie had given her
a liberated plum mouth,
lifting her brows
into permanent awareness—
when from an old MGM movie, she started to sing,
"Love is Where You Find It." None of us knew
that Marty could sing. Blinking
her azure lids and sapphire lashes,
she sat at her old schoolteacher desk,
just singing her heart out
like Kathryn Grayson. But I heard
Marty sing for the bruises
on my grandmother's face
from the beatings my grandfather gave.

And Marty sang the blues for my mother,
who paints on sorrow
in the slash of her mouth
and retrograde brows. For years,
she sneaked across the chill dawn floor
for more rouge and lipstick, coaxing
black waves and spit-curls into her hair—
before laying perfection back beside my father,
who was too snoring-full of whiskey to care.

But then Marty's running high C
trebled for my volcanic Aunt Helen,
who made Depression air sing
by vaulting her ironing board
to scatter the bully she'd wed
like pumice and ash
through a screen door. So I waited
for Marty to sing me into somebody
who can roll from bed without groping
first thing for mascara. Yet I lifted
my face to Cassie as if to the sun,
longing to watch makeovers all night—
planes sculpted with concealer and shadow,
released blooming with blush.

TO MOTHER, AGE 76, AS SHE SKY-DIVES

> —*Look around you . . .*
> *The Surviving Bull*

Leave in the plane's belly
those nights when your mother
waited in the dark
to harm you. Grieve before
you soar from your childhood
into lark-song. Keep your back
to Youngstown as you
step onto the wheel
and grip the strut. Try not
to hold your breath, and when
the Skymaster shouts, "Let go!"
                  allow the sky to cradle you
                          during the opening shock
                                  of substantial sensory air.

Overhead, the plane's diminishing.
Diminished. Now there are only currents
                  the tips of your sneakers,
                        and earth rushing toward you . . .
Put on blue and yellow,
be joined by snap of silk to sun and sky
as you scan Ohio country roads
for the farmhouse you tended as a bride.
Right there, wrench from your heart
what makes you tired. Just let it

fall. Your bad leg won't hurt so much
during this passage more upwind
than anything you've ever known
as you steer your toggles
toward safe ground . . .

Look, can you see us three kids
guiding you in with outstretched arms?

ON THE WAY TO PUMP IRON AT TULLY'S

—I felt death straining . . .
The Speared Horse

Beyond Crusade Baptist Church, shrubless, ready,
and Guardian Angels Catholic Church with its
trimmed evergreens and emerald lawn,
there's the small gray church that weighed
us down—where you served, husband,
and we shared footsteps as true
as Martin Luther's to that Wittenberg door
by mouthing doctrine into morning—
until I confused you with God,
your preacher-finger pointing me
for thirteen years toward Ephesians 5:22.*

Now there's less between us than crabgrass
on the Baptists' lawn. On my lawn
a black swan molts her feathers, slaked
by any love left in this world at all. Here
are two feathers, one for your new wife;
I'll shed the rest down at Tully's
where I can feel to my core the crash
of weights, deafening and right,
to what sweats from my pores.

I have a body to build while there's time
in a dim spartan room where men treat women
with shy relief, where fatigue and faith marry
amid raw grunts and groans. But
the barbell's a husband, who takes too long,
pressed above my arched pecs, straining.

*(Wives, be obedient to your husbands as if to the Lord.)

Muscles gird where abs once flubbed and triceps
sighed, yet there's a vastland where buttocks
have relinquished the fight. I have dead lifts
to perfect for when I awaken, scared, nights,
and squats under such weighted shoulders
gluts burn from the essential tearing, that I can
scarcely rise. For this, I disappear into thunder,
emerging pumped up, pared down, immortal.

DAVIDA AND I CHECK OUT SAKS

—I would have burst into five constant stars . . .
The Victim of Flames

Stuart said spend three hundred dollars,
he'd add to her eighty, but his indulgence
makes Davida grip her purse tighter
as she twirls in English flower garden
ascending with lace by Laura Ashley:
hyacinth, foxglove, and every primrose
I ever knew. *Too fussy*, she rules,
choosing beige linen, nine ninety-five,
no label. It does turn her into tall
blond wheat, and yes, she can dress it up,

she can dress it down, I agree next door
at the gourmet deli where bean salad spills
forward like agates. During apricot mousse,
we know we can't put this day down
like plastic utensils, we dash
back inside Saks, sashay in Chanel suits
and felt hats. We swing crocodile handbags
dyed astonishing colors, ogling
ourselves often in mirrors—faces by
Princess Marcella Bourghese. Our mouths
fall open, Dior slipping through gloved fingers.
If shoppers stare, we're pleased they freeze
and stay out of our way as we gather to us
billows of beaded silk scarves and suede belts,
so soft we're, briefly, silent. Oh, look at us!

We're tapestry, we're leopard, we're pin-striped,
we're Venus wistfully afloat on one shrewd sea.
Surely we've drawn security's eye,
yet nobody stops us. We paw on—
perfumed by Paloma—disdaining
a basket overflowing with chiffon cabbage rose
jewelry, marked pathetically down
as we frenzy toward Saks' arched door

until, who knows, we could buy the whole
darn store, then bored, bring it back.

ACT 1: SPRING

—Flower blooming from my broken sword.
The Dismembered Warrior

The silk woman is moving back in,
she has returned to her bud-green beginnings.

Listen, do you hear the tumult she causes,
crackling her ripe life? Stamping, she spins

into passion, this woman, clapping
and swirling. She transports her history

in a potpourri jar. She hurls
primary petals toward complementary skies,

her past rising and falling in her currents
like feathers, weary and brave.

Whooping, she leaps over claw marks and ashes.
Look, she has swaddled herself

in gamboge burstings, in magenta
and deep periwinkle, coloring the bog.

JUMPING FROM THE HAYLOFT

—Some damn fool bird singing its heart out.
The Surviving Bull

The hay-sweet air rushes to meet me
as I sneak into the barn. Sunbeams through slats
dapple the new owner's cows as I scale
the loft ladder, peer out the open loft door
at the lawn where Grandpa and I
paused by peonies so heavy they bent
in a pale pink lather to the ground. Right there,
he would swoop me through the air like a circus star
before we gathered the wild gifts of summer:
Queen-Anne's-lace with deep purple hearts,
bluets bunched with yarrow like tiny dropped stars.
Beyond are the orchards where we rode
his tractor early mornings when mist
still hung in the apple trees.

Now the fruit is knobby, worm-ridden,
gone to weeds the ruthless strawberry fields
that stole my grandparents lives,
forcing my family to move
from their farmhouse apartment
into a square house with pickle-green shutters
built by my father with no place to hide,
no solace for me except this barn.

"Get ready down there!" I holler. Cows stop chewing
their cud to gaze upward with soft startled eyes.
One lifts her head and bawls, setting off a moo-chorus.
Another shifts its body and a stirring sweeps down the line
as if they've been waiting for me to perk up their lives.
Gripping the rope, I count to twelve for the apostles,
and swing out fast, letting go . . .
                    then, oh, that
                        plummeting
                            split-second
                                when I'm cradled by air . . .

before chuting exuberantly down the haystack
arms outstretched like a trapeze artist—
just as if my bare feet won't meet
the dirt floor brain-joltingly hard,
and my legs will never betray me
by straying into more loss.

With Thanks

For all the poets who have shaped me, starting with dear Mildred Durham at Northwestern Community College, Geri Radacsi & Wood Thrush Poets, Brendan Galvin, Bernice Mennis, Mary Carroll Moore, Jessica Treat, Honor Moore, The Frost Place, Vermont College, and the wonderful Beekley Community Library Writing Workshop with Linda, Denise, Jack, Kiersten & Michele.

Morgan Baylog Finn cleaned houses, did makeovers, and sold biodegradable laundry soap on Cape Cod—whatever it took to earn her B.A. in creative writing from Vermont College. Her publishing credits include *Crab Creek Review, Jane's Stories, Tallgrass, poemmemoirstory, South Florida Review, Kalliope, Thema,* and *Castings.* One piece was dramatized by Connecticut Public television in conjunction with Wood Thrush Poets and the CT Commission on the Arts to help open poetry to a wider audience.

After viewing Picasso's gut-wrenching mural at The Modern, none of Finn's poetry ever took more time or focus than "Guernica." Since then, it grew from a maudlin poem into a seven-part dramatic monologue. Picasso said, "The public who look at the picture must interpret the symbols as they understand them." After much research, her goal in *The Gathering* was to depict the Basque people, especially when she saw poignant correlations to the abuses in her own family who—because of the irony of time and place—had a chance to deal with their troubled lives. Guernica became more than just shared characteristics, Finn's fears emerging in "The Despairing Woman" separated from her daughter, the trauma of a neglected relative in "The Woman in Flames," and the vulnerability of animals.

www.ingramcontent.com/pod-product-compliance
Lightning Source LLC
Chambersburg PA
CBHW020221090426
42734CB00008B/1169